TRP DESCANT FOR HELMSLEY (R.B. # 393)

B♭ TRP DESCANT FOR ASCENSION (R.B #153)(Playor vs 1 & 4)

B♭ TRP DESCANT FOR STUTTGART (RB #389) Play 2 rt

Written "Fri night, when I couldn't sleep"?
27 - 28 Nov 1992
by William Barnes

Complex
Variables

poems &
music by

William John Barnes

Edited by David Helwig and Peter Taylor

Quarry Press

The editors would like to thank the many colleagues, and friends and family of Bill for their support of this project. In particular we will mention Janice Coles for her careful copying of the music, Lisa Miller and Cathy Barnes for conversations and photographs, Olive Juby for the page of handwritten music displayed on the cover, and the Departments of English and Mathematics & Statistics at Queen's University for their technical support.

The publisher gratefully acknowledges the support of The Canada Council, the Department of Canadian Heritage, and the Ontario Publishing Centre.

Canadian Cataloguing in Publication Data is available.

ISBN 1–55082–128–8

Graphic Design: Peter Dorn RCA, FGDC.

Printed and bound in Canada by Hignell Printing, Winnipeg, Manitoba.

Published by Quarry Press, Inc.,
P.O. Box 1061, Kingston, Ontario K7L 4Y5.

CONTENTS

FOR BILL,
IN APRIL

The body is the first dream, and music
is the second, while the landscape
of love waits in vast silence
like the far darkness of the spring night.

Health and song and rare words,
the power of thought, all these, old friend,
the luck of the draw. Choices
fall into our lap like a basket of stars.

And God deliver us from goodness:
save us for the commonplace quotidian,
the falling body, this dream
that allows us to share laughter.

David Helwig

Sometime in the early 1980s I was looking for someone to help me teach
a "math and poetry" course, and George Logan led me down the hall to
Bill's office, and it was strange how there were really no preliminaries at
all – as if we both knew right away we were going to do it. Indeed, the
title of this book reflects a fascination Bill had with mathematical things.
It was a phrase he picked up somewhere in a math book (it's also the
title of a third year math course), and I can see him smile when he came
across it, further evidence that mathematicians have answers to big
questions. Anyway, when he played with the idea that some day he
might collect together some of his poems (already collected in a corner of
his office in a cardboard box), *Complex Variables* was the title he
thought he would use.

In fact, mathematicians do have answers to big questions, but that
might be because they choose very special kinds of questions. Bill would
delight at seeing these answers emerge from the class at the end of the
math hour, simple, beautiful, compelling, unexpected, (pardon this brief
self-indulgence) and he'd shake his head and say "well, well..." He
proposed a number of times that I should do a class on chaos,
wondering if perhaps there'd be even a corner of that which could yield
a simple elegant answer.

And when it was my turn to sit in the class and watch, I in turn
would delight at seeing the poem emerge, analyzed, trodden on,
reinvented, now read again at the end, and in some magic way given a

new life – the same poem we started with, but so much more. That's a kind of answer right there, and Bill must have often felt it was the only kind of answer his questions would ever get.

> ...Wondered, like Milton, the usual
> why? And found, like him,
> no answer save the poem.

The struggle that Bill waged on many levels, moral, emotional, spiritual, intellectual, physical (most of all physical?) resonates in these poems, and is often the occasion for the poem itself. Art which is born of anguish must surely temper it. And you will discover in these pages that much of his art came from his wondering at the world, and his joy in being part of that, a joy that is heard most clearly in his music and hymns.

What else should I say? He was the only instructor in the Faculty of Arts and Science to win the ASUS (the undergraduate society) teaching award twice, an honour he valued highly because the award comes from the students themselves. In his last year he was also awarded a prestigious 3M Teaching Fellowship. He represented the NDP Party in the provincial elections in 1975 and 1977, the second time, struggling with footsores that refused to heal and periodic bouts of poor eyesight. Can you imagine him canvassing in that state from door to door...? For some twenty years he was choirmaster and organist at St James' Anglican Church, and the music we include was all written during this period.

He was honoured and delighted to have been asked to write the Queen's Sesquicentennial Hymn. The music seemed to come quickly enough, but for sometime he played restlessly with the words, looking for a way to capture the breadth of his scholarly fascinations – art, literature, science, human behaviour. The inaugural performance of the hymn was at St Andrew's Presbyterian Church at the Sesquicentennial Service on October 16, 1991, just over a year before he died. When the time came for the hymn he stood tall and sang out somewhat louder than is considered polite in the midst of a large well-dressed Southern Ontario congregation. A man standing in front of him turned half around with a frown, but the woman beside him nudged him back into line: "He wrote the hymn," she whispered in his ear.

People often wondered if the math and poetry course was about structure and metre and mathematical limericks, but of course it wasn't at all. Over the years we both discovered that it was about many different things to many different students, but for me, it was about standing together and reaching, each one of us, into the depths of some professional reservoir, and getting the same class in the same evening to talk to us and to one another about what we produced.

But the course had a significance for me that went beyond that: my work with Bill erected new standards for my life as a mathematics teacher. An hour spent with a John Updike poem struggling with love and loss ("Love it now./Love it now, but we can't take it home."), or a Robert Frost poem delivered in the sonorous Barnes-Frost voice (Nature's first green is gold/Her hardest hue to hold.) – what mathematics problem what numerical exploration, what geometric trick, can presume to follow such an experience? A standard was set, and I was constantly struggling to measure up. I take that struggle with me today into every course I teach.

Okay, he'd say, let's array the forces, and he'd draw a vertical line down the middle of the board. That was high entertainment for me, and I'd watch fascinated as the class argued about which side a certain word or phrase belonged to, or whether it dared to be classified at all: light/darkness, joy/sadness, Apollo/Dionysus. It was the last pair of categories that was the most compelling for me as I struggled in my own life to let go of a life-long allegiance to Apollo. Bill was well acquainted with that struggle:

> I sit upon the rock-face, which is being
> assaulted by the waves' hammering,
> admiring as always
> the stability of anything stable
> (worrying at the same time also
> about the relentlessness of water in motion).

Perhaps he did admire the stability of stable things, but I don't doubt that his real fascination was for the swirling of the water. Certainly his own being, emotional and physical, was always assaulted by the waves, and he understood that most forms of stability were not for him. Later in that same poem, we find flowers growing in the cracks along the rock.

He coped with a lot – eyesight that came and went, infections that came and wouldn't go, one leg, then the other, that deserted him, kidneys that let him down, and that's just the physical stuff...

> but you will someday come
> to know there is with me
> a history of awkwardness.

How can he cope?

> So for the moment
> I accept your terms.

I've not had to cope with such stuff myself, but even so, when things seem too much for me, I know I have to get out, to walk fast and far, or to run. But wheel-chair bound, he seemed so imprisoned in his small house.

> ...no more than room
> enough for even your small body, cramped
> and awkward, as the others tie down the lid,
> the cut edges of reeds pricking your flesh.

That's Bill settling with a sigh into his chair, scraping his knuckles again and again trying to wheel himself quickly enough through the heavy Watson Hall door. I take heart in recalling that the basket of reeds was actually a vehicle of freedom.

> ...the guts of friends are ropes paid out
> to let you down and set you free again.

But the double meaning in let you down has always stabbed at me. There were times that last fall when I was not there...

This last winter I taught the course for the first time without him, and got wonderful help from a number of his friends and colleagues. Three of the classes I took myself, nervous, thinking he must surely somehow be watching, taking courage from that. In perhaps my best class we worked with a couple of Marge Piercy poems which he had never used, but which I had found in a book on his office shelf. Let's array the forces! I said, and drew a line down the centre of the board.

Watching him, I might try to gauge what it was that made him such a beloved teacher. He was not always kind and easy – often he was impatient and even rude. His ritual treatment of a student who was unlucky enough to be late and wander in halfway through a poem he was reading aloud always made me uncomfortable. He would stop abruptly and stare at the offender in silence as he made his awkward way to his seat. I would have tended to be forgiving, to minimize the disturbance, to be annoyed but to carry on. But for Bill the process was sacred. Whatever he was doing was done with his entire being – he was there and expected nothing less of his students.

I should explain why that was significant to me. You see, in science teaching, there is often a tendency to depersonalize the process, to somehow stand aside and let the subject matter speak for itself. Perhaps that's even sometimes true in the humanities; indeed a colleague of mine in Religion once declared that he felt it his duty as a teacher to keep his own feelings about the work being studied to himself. But it was always clear how Bill felt about a poem, and I think the students appreciated that and responded to it. I think it did not intimidate or prejudice them because his directness and honesty evoked the same in them. And he didn't intrude (except with his awful jokes which I more than anyone else had to endure year after year – except I rather liked his pig jokes, one in particular...) So perhaps I've learned (or am trying to learn) to let my students know about my feelings towards a mathematical theorem, in a strange way it may give them an alternative context in which to find understanding. We often forget that science is first of all a human endeavour, and only secondly a corpus of results.

We end this collection with a poem that always moves and often perplexes me. Surely here he comes down firmly on the side of Dionysus – he prays that his young daughter will not hide from that sea wind that so worried Yeats as it screamed upon the tower where his small daughter was asleep. Let her not

> ...encase in the wrappings of carefulness
>   Her heart
> When it later moves
> As naturally as it does now
>   In curiosity and affection.
>
> Let her rather take the wind
>   For company...

Bill wondered, agonized, cursed, exalted, but most of all wondered, at the profound ambiguity of life: a spring song that does not sound like spring at all but more like fall.

> Under a disturbing sun, the trees are leaving again.
> Elements quicken towards another ending.

What he asked of himself, and what he asked of us, his lovers, friends, and colleagues, was simple and direct:

> But for the present I can hope that you will, through the madness
> Undertake the cherishing
> Not turn away.

Peter Taylor
September 1993

MY DAUGHTER CRIES

My daughter cries at midnight:
She does not know the animal
That crashes and pursues her
Through the shadows of her tiny head.

My daughter cries at midnight:
She does not recognize
The vague and threatening shapes
That beckon and withdraw
Behind the shadows of her infant fright.

And we who hear her
Hold our anxious silences:
We know that in the morning
Shadows die
And she will give us then
Her smile.

FORMAL POSE

You are my Irish grandfather,
and my childhood memories of you
are of a slightly stooped tall old man,
grey hair cropped close in a brush-cut,
a grey no-nonsense moustache accenting
your ready smile, and how you would
on every visit ask me to bike uptown
to buy the six White Owl cigars.

But here you are,
in this posed photograph my mother has given me,
seated on a straight-backed chair,
your hands not quite joined on your lap –
a young man, perhaps twenty-five,
with dark brown hair and a moustache waxed
and curled jauntily upward.
The effect is dashing:
a wing-collar and bow-tie on the man
I always imagined in a farmer's
rough clothing.

Stove-pipe pants without cuffs
in the prevailing mode: one leg
is crossed over the other, the toe
of its polished boot pointing
confidently forward. (The other foot
rests on what looks like
a bear-skin rug.)

D.E. Pelton & Son, Photographers,
of Kemptville and Merrickville,
circa 1895 have arranged the conventional
scenery: at your right arm
some indeterminate piece of furniture
has been draped with a white lace cloth;
to your left is a sturdy, square
four-legged table uncovered,
with a clutch of illegible papers
on its surface, and what may be
a Bible on the lower shelf.

The painted background offers the illusion
of green plants and fretted windows
hinting at an outside world.
The tones are all of brown
(like those in Joyce's Dublin)
in the way of these old photos.

In your young face the strong eyes
beneath the high forehead and dark eye-brows
seem to betray only a slight self-
consciousness, a vague apprehension
of the flash and smoke to come;
but the most direct impression
is of assurance, the quiet
steadiness of what my children
would call a "very together
person." Did you ever
realize this?

Nothing here tells me anything about
the occasion. How did you come
to sit for this (to me incongruous)
picture? I wish I could have
shown it to you while you were here
and asked what prompted
this curious solemnity, this sepia-
tinted seriousness. Whose eyes
were intended to see you thus?

You are my Irish grandfather:
Jack Connerty, born Pulaski, New York,
about 1870, railroad worker in the
Kicking Horse Pass, then cheese maker, then farmer,
then widower. You were gone
before I knew enough to know
what to ask; and now all I have
is this photograph and a few memories
still current in the one blood
connection: your daughter, my mother.

You are my Irish grandfather.
From you I get my height, my slight
build, perhaps (I never saw it in you)
an Irish temper, perhaps in some
roundabout way (it suddenly occurs to me)
my love of ceremony, of Yeatsian rituals,
perhaps my preference for life
on a farm, perhaps a certain
restlessness.

But what else? What else?
Out of this studied arrangement of browns
you look straight at me
and say nothing.

June 1989

AUNT EVA

Once (I might have been eight, or ten, or eleven) at the cottage
there was a thunderstorm, heavy
black clouds gathering strength in a hot August
afternoon: she went outside to shutter
the big screens against the flailing rain,
came back in, her huge body dripping and warm, said
it would be all right, the so-good smell of her filling
the place, taking away the fear; and she got out
the always-there doughnuts, and we waited together,
listening and watching until the storm passed:

But before that even: sliding summers full
of swimming and pancakes, watersnakes and brown sugar,
to sleep with the sound of frogs of all ages
and wake next morning to start the climb:
between the bedrooms were the old partitions that didn't reach
to the ceiling, the thin walls of heavily painted pine sheeting
into which the nails had been driven to hold
coat-hangers, empty and rattling or quietly supporting
the freshly ironed clothes; and I
would scramble and tug my way up,
the nail-heads gnawing into my belly, arms aching
from the strain, and reaching the top look down
to see her there, waiting as always for me to jump
into her creaking bed with its old-time quilts and covers, then
crawl in with her to be held and held, my face
pressed into that warm expansive flesh, with its funny smell,
while I listened again to the story about the little
boy who went to stay with his aunt at her cottage.

It was always good, like that: later,
in Toronto, she bought the Black Watch
tartan vest with the gold
buttons for the too-bright
college student trying so hard
to be cool, his head
full of Aristotle, heart mostly
wanting.

Then she returned to Kemptville, back
home (my visits only a small
handful, Christmas or summer),
and she retired – the spinster
school-teacher with the sallow eyes
and warm smile; and I sit
in her second-storey apartment,
(for the moment, a failed marriage
and three children my only
accomplishments) and try
to tell her my confused
tale, to explain
the unexplainable. And in the course
of this, I see her profound
innocence, and hear her say:
"And what's impotence, Bill?"

And later still:
the hospital bed with its white
sterility, the narrow room
smelling of disinfectant, she
lying there enduring the dark cancer
which gradually took away
her insides so that
on my successive
visits I watched
that immense body grow
smaller and smaller until
there was almost nothing
left for death to take;
and I told her I wished
I could stop it – but
bending close to her parched
lips, I heard her strained voice
say: "I don't think
there's anything
anybody can do
for me now, Bill."

And then
on a day
in November
(I was not there)
her story
ended.

July/August 1982

MARY McCLUSKEY

For Kemptville in the 1950s she was
something else again: a woman who dressed
in a man's clothing always, went everywhere
(Sundays or work-days) wearing the tough,
thick-soled leather boots, the hard-textured twill
pants, three or four rough plaid shirts, the forage
cap (the ear-flaps turned down against the cold
in winter).

Even the face was mannish – at times suggesting
the indeterminate look of a department store
mannequin: smooth, unblemished forehead
and cheeks and nose, these latter almost unnaturally
red, like those of a clown or puppet.
Steel-rimmed glasses protected eyes which
alternately drew and held your gaze
with fiery concentration or else wandered
around or through you uncomprehending.

People were curiously accepting of all this.
Let Mary be. We would hear, almost without remark
or judgment, that Mary was working
as a farm-hand just outside of town,
throwing the heavy hay-bales onto the wagon
with the strength of any able-bodied male.
Or we discovered that she had joined
the town garbage crew, sometimes lifting
the cans or tied boxes up to the man
in the back of the open dump-truck, sometimes
scrambling around in the truck herself, grabbing
and emptying the containers, almost contemptuously
flinging the pails and lids back down
to the men below.

Later, at the dump-site after the day's
run she would remain behind
when the truck and crew had gone back
to town. The boys who had been
shooting rats with a .22 would see her
there as she clambered over the mounds of refuse,
picking up this or that, examining, pondering,
then discarding or pocketing her discoveries. She
ignored the rats, refused
to acknowledge even our presence with more
than an occasional side-long glance.

Soon it seemed to us that she came
nearly every day, as if scavenging
had become her vocation, as if she
were driven now to sift and sort through
other people's leavings, as if she hoped
that each new occasion, each new
performance of the ritual, would yield up
the ultimate, extraordinary treasure.

Observing her at this, day after day,
some of us began to wonder,
from the way she seemed never satisfied,
how she would ever know if she
found it.

May 1983

FOR KEITH,
WHO DIED OF DRINK

In those days we had bottles:
half-pints, pints, quarts, all banging crazily
in their wood and wire cages.
Cream, chocolate, white, this last
only "pasturized," not yet homogenized.
Mostly I remember the noise, the noise
at the jerky starts and stops, the almost incessant
rattling of bottles, occasionally
the dull "thuck" and surprised "pop"
of a full one dropped on pavement
or the brilliant metallic
explosion of an empty as it shattered
on the dairy floor,

When I started with you we had
the horse, too: in the summer the quiet rubber-tired
wagon, in winter the sleigh with its twin
sets of steel runners. In the worst
of winter, the deep cold would push
the cream up and out the necks, tipping
the paper lids in a series
of rakish doorstep greetings.
But the horse, the horse both was and was not
its own cliche: it knew where and when
to stop and start, knew that when your weight
and mine hit the wagon together it was time
to move on. Occasionally he would be overtaken
by a will of his own, would saunter down
the street, even where there was no
roadside grass to draw him on,
until one of us raced after him and caught
the reins.

Sometimes, with an abiding calm, he waited
in the hard cold of early dawn
while we huddled with coffee around the old
cast-iron wood-stove in the hotel
kitchen. Sometimes in summer he and I
waited together while you dallied, talking
with some woman inside the house
or shifting your weight at the screen door
or backing slowly and awkwardly
across the lawn to the cart
and our getaway.
     Looking out past the horse's
     rump and back and ears, I knew only my own
     restlessness to get done for the day,
     could not grasp all the meaning
     of these visits, the subtle discriminations.

Then we got our first truck:
the red Ford van with the gearshift
on the steering column, unheard of for trucks
in those days. It knew nothing, of course,
had to be started and shifted and steered
and stopped. But on it I learned
to drive, and got my licence,
and took over some and then more and more
of the driving.

Sometimes I *had* to drive
(at first it was mainly at Christmas
or New Year's) because your friends
or even the housewives would offer you "cheer,"
the men waving us over, sidling
up to us, furtively or openly
pulling out the flask or the 26er,
handing it to you
      – later even to me,
      the raw liquor screaming
      down my throat, defeating my futile
      attempts to brave it out, to pretend
      I could take it –
until with maybe ten or twelve
such rituals your eyes would cloud, your tongue
would slow, your rubber legs would turn you into
the stereotype of the laughable drunk.

      You did not deserve this.
      You had given me my first-ever job,
      had forgiven my clumsy days when every tenth
      bottle slid madly out of my grasp and broke,
      You had helped me to learn what little I was
      stumbling upon about the world and people.
      You had eased my entrance into the mysteries
      of work and adults.

And away from work: Saturday nights, coming
home from a dance with my first
girl, I would watch your car
lurch around a downtown Kemptville
corner (you had your wife with you, maybe
another couple), or see you
stopped, still on the roadway,
your window down, your head
lolling out, your voice raucous but slurred:
"Hey, Bill! C'mon over. I need
to talk to ya." But then you would
roar off into the dark.

It's been almost thirty years now,
From time to time I would hear
about you from my parents: how
your brother had sold the milk business,
how your wife had left you, come back,
left again. You were working
as a prison guard, showing up incapable,
in danger of losing your job, then
losing it. "He's not too good"
my mother would say. Or, "they tell me he's worse,"
my father would say.

Then on my last visit home
to Kemptville, I found out
that you'd died, whatever of you
that was left having drifted
gradually further and further away
from the wasted body on the narrow
white hospital bed.

It was inevitable, I guess;
it was not as if I didn't know
it would come sooner or later.
Still, for all I've learned
between that time and now,
I cannot grasp the sense
of such a death.

For the moment,
I can only
stop here, waiting
for some signal
to move on.

May 1983

ON THE DEATH OF MY FATHER

At the wake they told the story
Of how one Sunday afternoon in August
(you were about 60)
the people at the cottage next door
had a power boat and water skis
and were parading on the river –

of how, stirred by a drink
or your own impishness,
you declared that you
not only wanted
but fully intended
to go water-skiing
(never mind that you'd never
done it before),

and how they relented and let you try,
setting up the wide boards by the dock,
handing you the tow-line,
which you held with both
your strong-willed hands.

Then the sudden surge of the engine:
you were yanked away. In an instant
you lost the skis
to the grab of the water,
went down under the surface
for 50 feet or so
and then appeared again,
a green creature covered in river-weed,
gasping and puffing
but clinging still to the rope-tow.
(No one had explained
about letting go.)

Just another tale to liven up
a languid summer day, I suppose,
no doubt embellished in the telling,

but I want to read it now as prophecy,
hinting at some other passage
where you emerge to find yourself
in a final radiant greening
and a fine applause of light,

holding on
to the laughter of friends.

June 1988

THE KNACK

Milton found it usually
In the early morning
(Especially at Christmastime)
Unless he tells a lie
For the sake of prettiness
Or truth.

I say it comes late,
Late in darkness,
Though with the same fluency, perhaps,
But I have nothing pretty
For it to be for the sake of.

Still, I'm grateful.

Advent Anthem

W. J. Barnes

Good Friday Anthem

W. J. Barnes

Good Friday 2

January 1970

FOR HENRY VAUGHAN

My soul, not far from here
There dwells, I'm told, a country
Where orange trees blossom from the pavement
Thistles bleed milk
And young children direct empires,
Legislating wild and beautiful rivers.

In that place
Sentries in red tunics and white hats
Provide security by night
Against the ravages of grass
And the temptations of contraception,
Wielding their joyfulness with precision.

No man need love there
And William Blake will preside
Over contingents of serpents
And wild goats
While Milton reads his biographies,
Harbouring neither regret nor rancor.

And there (I hear) my limbs
Will seek their loves
Among dancing gardens
And (if what I hear is true)
Choirs of silken rats will sing
In solemn panegyric,
Liberating the houses and the streets alike.

Perhaps some homes will be deserted
Because of the danger
But retreat will be discouraged
With roses,
And smiling constellations
Will give public entertainments skilfully.

But why then does my heart refuse,
Clasping hesitant flowers?

Is it fear or Joy
That whispers this firm command,
Urging restraint with fine phrases?

Is it the daemon of confusion
Or the genius of place
Prevents me?

O grave and strenuous Henry,
I am not ready.
I am not ready.

WAITING FOR
THIS POEM ABOUT WAYMAN

In 1973 the backside dust-Jacket
of Waiting for Wayman displayed
a photograph of Wayman (or one
of his many selves) posing naked
to the waist (which is as far
as we can see) save for a thick-
banded wrist-watch, a ring on one
finger, and thin (I mean thin)
steel-framed eye-glasses.

The chest is dark with hair,
the watch is ticking quietly, and the head
is turned ever so slightly, the eyes
gently concentrated, smiling on us
as we observe them. The thick hair,
the full moustache and beard, are black
as the ink hardly anyone uses any more.
The nose is strong, Judaic.

Though the right arm is mostly
outside the picture, the feeling we get
is that he's flexing his muscle, checking
its bulge with the other hand
in the way of adolescent boys.
(Does Wayman use weights?)

But that's not all:
the photographer's backdrop
is another photo, this one of
– what? That first indelible
surreal mushroom cloud over Hiroshima?
Or the rippled convoluted grey
matter of a human brain, its stem
depending behind Wayman's own head?

Hard to tell. Like the slightly elfish look
on Wayman's face, this utterance staged
by double agents is gnomic. Has it something
to do with the power of the poet, a rawness
like that of the naked poser? Is it poetry
as prophetic realism in a bad time?
Language ordered to explode: destroying
old worlds to create anew? (See Yeats's
rough and slouching beast.)
Who knows?

Who knows? The watch on Wayman's arm
continues ticking, ticking. For 15 years now,
whenever I've read to my students

from this poetry of love and work
and death, I've pointed to this
jacket photograph, and said there was
a poem in there somewhere and I'd
a mind to write it.

Why has it taken so long?
From the worn surface of this
black and white photo, Wayman
flashes his cryptic smile.
So long.

June 1989

ON CORKUM'S ISLAND
For Bonnie & Steve Frick

On the Atlantic side, the island
lifts easily from the shore to the house
and behind the house to the road
and beyond. Aggressive or gentle,
the wind from the east off the sea
almost never stops shoving or nudging
the house, which holds its own.

Together they have designed it,
and Steve has built it snug
with his own large hands and those
of friends: they have raised
the heavy posts and beams to clear
spaces almost everywhere for the light,
leaving behind the insistent scent
of raw wood to sleep with at night.

On the outside, the walls
are covered with the golden armor-plate
of cedar shakes stapled on
with a power-gun. This is
no antique being restored but a new
construction raised on unsettled ground,
ready to face two centuries of sea-winds,
should they come.

Inside, the solarium embraces
the kitchen where Bonnie and Lisa
make our meals; clusters
of spice-plants hang from hooks.
And always, eating or drinking
or driving to Lunenberg, we have
the conversations which leap like inspired
dancers from serious talk to silly chatter
and back in the twinkling of a synapse.

Later we will stretch out
on cushions and blankets in the loft,
drinking beer and watching the Expos
lose again in that summer of '82.

(My eyesight that year is too dim to catch
the ball off the bat or even to follow
the base-runners, but the others take turns
giving me the play-by-play. The air
is thick with giddy cackles or cries
of "Shit, Bonnie, that's *three* strikes!")
(Another time, looking for some way
to help, I will offer to weed
Bonnie's flower gardens, though
in my darkness I will as often
pluck out flowers. No one minds.)

Later still, the island, this house
and this new-found family
(Bonnie and Steve have never met Lisa before)
will ride calmly in the moon's wash.
My dream will be of sunshine
in long grass and quiet waves
on a pebbled shore.

*

In the week they moved in,
the last of the Corkums to live
on this island named for their family
was buried: cantankerous old
Burton, who had drunk most
of a bottle of whiskey every day
for the last seven years. He would
come by and stand in his heavy farmer's boots
to watch Steve pour the foundations
or lift the heavy planks into place.
Or he would snore fitfully on a pile
of plywood or chat drowsily with that
"city feller from somewheres down in the States,
there, Colorado or somewhere."
Bonnie would bring him his tea.

Sometimes, coming home at night,
they would find him in his truck
by the side of the country road,
asleep with his head lolling back,
his nose pointing skyward, the headlights
still on, or sometimes the motor still
running, yet with an aura of vague
apprehension about him, as if he were
about to begin a crazy journey
driving the old Ford over tree-tops
and house-roofs, on past the island,
past the whole confounded mainland,
to some secret meeting in the sky.

*

Next day, the sun enters
its intended place. All of
Bonnie's plants turn to greet it.
They cock their green ears,
catching the ripples and short silences
of our morning-talk.

1982-89

BUDGIE AT THE BANK

They tell me no one knows
how he got in (sedately, on his owner's
shoulders? deftly, through an air-vent,
the lone escapee from a budgie wholesaler's
silent truckload?) but as I'm
standing at the teller's cage, I
suddenly find him there beside me,
balancing on a cardboard sign announcing
interest rates (9% is the best they can
do for us today): a lightly poised
display of black and white and bright
canary yellow, mostly
yellow...

The quick dark eyes inspect
a fluorescent underground
world, calculate the openings
and the risks

– then he pushes off to whirl and float
and dive in a round of easy curves
and straight near-misses, all
confined within the space
behind the counters. (Smart
bird, I say to myself.) The pert-
breasted Bank of Montreal girls flutter
variously in reactions of amusement,
curiosity or fright (somebody
has already called the Ministry
of Natural Resources):

"Aren't they supposed to talk
a lot?" "If he does it
on this new dress, I'll..." "He's gonna
send me to the hospital!" (This
from the twitchy victim of two
close-call passes.)

Unsettled, they go on
trying to do their jobs. But delicate
vague smiles and smuggled sideways
glances tell me that they're really half
taken with him...

Computers hum and click,
hum and click. ("You'll never
guess what happened
at work today, love...")

Later, going out the door,
I turn and catch sight
of the Conservation Officer
in his brown uniform: he has come
to take care of everything, armed
with a fish-net and a blue
plastic milk-case – both
with holes large enough
to make him a failure.
I guess he must
be used to taking
bigger things.

But for now
the wild thrill of yellow
has come to rest on the window-sill,
facing in toward us all. He has found
his voice, and he uses it
again and again.

July-August 1984

IKONOKLASTES

The morning all the idols cracked
I wrote myself a poem
That showed it really wasn't just
The way it was.

That poem said
That what had happened was
That other idols came
To take their place
And that the shifting made
Imaginary crumblings
Which I then mistook for dust.

But a poem doesn't fool me.
From time to time
I still can taste
From some deep cavity
A piece of grit.

EX CATHEDRA

Sitting here,
editing an established
literary magazine
from this narrow office,
playing God
as I send my judgments forth,
while my pipe keeps going out
as I pause to seal replies,

I am no longer amazed
at how I got here,

merely tired of being midwife
or a mediating priest
when what I want is act not ritual
and a kind of speech that matters
more than "yes" or "no,"

having got stuck
with licking
envelopes.

DAVID WRITING

Helwig's hair, in those days, seemed to fly
in all directions, sparked by a moving
static, charged to new accounts
of men and women playing out
the frets of their existence.

I would pass his office, glimpse
a vision of his rattling typewriter dancing
on the desk, with all the keys, it seemed,
aloft at once: illusion of entanglement
as keys and beard and hair-strands flew together
making tales of fire and of magic
and of love.

Now that he's gone,
I never get to see that anymore,
but I find myself imagining him –
wherever he does his amazing thing –
riding that ancient writing machine:

a man on fire with the love of things,
his hair all one with the silver keys,
and words like sunlight flashing out.

30 March 1982

DAVID BARTENDING

It's a bit like the picture in
"David Writing," except that it's
seven years later and there is
less hair and beard now,
and the illumination here comes
hardly at all from the pseudo-
twilight of this bar in The Grand
Theatre, and only a little from
the transient glints off glasses
and bottles. The light is in the eyes,
which seem to ask for something more
than your order, and offer
even more.

And the old magic is still
around: turning to the fridge he grows
two dark brown bottles from
the ends of his hands, like a juggler's
clubs, and in an instant they have
landed, hats off, on the bar-top,
with two upside-down glasses covering
their throats – all this without
his hands ever moving from
their first position on the oak
and vinyl keyboard of the bar.
There has been one
fluid, almost audible
swoo-oo-oosh amid the noisy
chatter of this intermission. It is
a service unlike any other,
a performance hardly anyone
notices.

When the drinks have turned
ordinary again, you look up
from the bar to find the eyes
holding you once more, and
the voice grins and says: "That'll be
three dollars."

You pay him the money, which he
flicks flamboyantly into the cash.
(There is no tall hat or cape that
you can see.)

He moves on
down the line. "Can I
help you?" he asks. "Next?"

Next?

1989

a sort of a songette for tommy

there he is   yes   he is there
tommy   yes   tommy
his name now at least
on my brand new file-
folder   merry, his name
in blue
ink, in Mary-blue-ink: my hope-
folder, then, hoping
to con-
tain him, keep his cor-
respondence (core-spondence?) in
keep   it in   en-
folder him, get him into
place
   (his letters and poems and
stuff)   in
place   yes

        but
        he won't stay there
            all the
            pages climbing out
            smiling & flying off
            waving, grinning

hold on here   hold on
organize   organize

        but
        he always grows a
        way out ...

fold then   en-
fold him:
his art stuff   heart stuff

heart-fold, then, a heart-
felt folding, fold him
in arms, in hands fold, in
heart hold   him

he always breaks out
(though he never did, in fact,
ex-con-
victed)
can't be pre-con-
ceived

o.k.   then
put it all in
there: little heaps   (no hoops,
mind, no
hoops)

of heaven-hope for the
hope-hungry and hammering
world; weary
as I am I try

to put it all
in there
folder him
shoulder him
down

when I have it
all in there (letters, poems, 'n stuff)
especially the letters from,
out of his always un-
prison
I will have it then yes:
the key to his
never actually but always
breaking
out ...

no! it can't be
con-
centrated in there, it's more
outside, here in him-
self, con-
secrated in his wonderful
goings & doings, fro-ings &
to-ings which
strangely help my hope-
hold
   (hand-hold and touch, touch)

which is here now and being
here now, here holds

it holds

it does ...

   but gently, gently

and o my God yes so
loose!

Post - Communion Anthem

W. J. Barnes

Soprano: Who by thy Cross - and

Alto: Who by thy Cross - and

Tenor: O Sav - iour Christ who by thy Cross and pre - cious Blood ... Who by thy

Bass: Who by thy Cross and pre - cious Blood

pre — cious Blood — Hast re - deemed us — Hum - bly we a - dore Thee.

pre — cious Blood — Hast re - deemed us — Hum - bly we a - dore Thee.

pre — cious Blood — Hast re - deemed us — Hum - bly we a - dore Thee.

who — by thy Blood — Hast re - deemed us — Hum - bly we a - dore Thee,

Rockhold

W. J. Barnes (June 1991)

Queen's University Sesquicentennial Hymn

Majestically – not too fast

1. To the Auth-or of our wind-ing sto-ry —— Let us raise to-day our grate-ful song ——
—, Watch-ing still for signs of fut-ure glo-ry —— Yet to rise on deep foun-da-tions strong —— .

2. As we meditate on old successes,
   May we contemplate tomorrow's course,
   Be a body that outright confesses
   Our dependence on sustaining Source.

3. When we scan dark interstellar spaces,
   When we chart the atom's lively core,
   When we fathom heart's or mind's large places,
   Let us sense, with awe, the Maker's store.

4. In the webs of circle, line and number,
   In the wreck of tissue, cell and nerve,
   In the face of virtue's seeming slumber,
   May we still embrace the Hope we serve.

5. Thus continuing in our former footsteps,
   Thus conjoining human and divine,
   We'll show forth our grasp of wisdom's precepts,
   Look to see the Light of learning shine.

W.J. Barnes (May 1991)

BIRTH POEM
for Ian Christopher

Yes of course:
after what seems
the long twisted river of blood,
we all come bearing the unmistakeable marks,
the imposing gifts, of apparent chance.

Yours (I hear) is voice:
a keen capacity to proclaim
the truths of pain, departure, hunger,
frustration, cold – harsh prophecies
that burn our hearts with images
of an ancient fiery hillside,
childhood calamities, the ravaged
man-in-the-next-bed, the cancer-
silenced baritone.

But push on still:
draw in more air in the suspenseful
pause, while we await
your next raw, piercing phrase.

we need to feel your sheer rage:
you are the poet, imagining
wildly, like all of us the disasters
voiced (however roughly) will make some kind
of sense, though still no less cross-
purposed –

  like all of us who tell ourselves,
in darkest whisper or bright cry,
it's safe enough
to answer "Yes."

January 1984

"Belly up to the bar, boy. It's time
you got what's coming to you. The red
rain is falling inside, inside. Trees
have turned into shadowy statues.
The flowers have all dis-
appeared. The windows are all
fogged up, all fogged up. Stumble on
over here. Bark your shins
on tables and chairs. Who did you think
you were anyway? It's time to toss
it back, toss it back."

And he did toss it back: into the face
of whatever fate was wrestling with him.
Until the eyes grew clear of blood-fall
he saw with fingers and ears, felt things
as if for the first time, listened
strenuously to the reading of friends
and students and wife, discovered
sixth and seventh senses to manage,
kept on teaching his classes, playing
the Sunday services ("by heart,"
as someone said), green circles glued
on the organ keys to mark the Cs,
cried a lot, into the bargain, under a dying
willow tree in the backyard, both
did and did not take it
on the lam, tried (like Milton)
to respond creatively and mostly
could. Wondered, like Milton, the usual
why? And found, like him,
no answer save the poem.

1982-1989

---

*Diabetic retinopathy causes blindness when the
cells at the back of the eye break down and
leak blood into the field of vision.

BEING IN HOSPITAL

Like war or travel or natural disaster,
it brings you face to face with
unfathomable questions, prods you
with the quirky particulars
of place and time, pinpoints
the enigmatic conjunction
and collapse of things,
sets self and family against all those other
random traditions, why
some people do things one way, some another, why
we are moved toward this one
or that. Or not.
It jostles you up against
an assortment of men and women,
some of whom you would like
to call "friend" forever but won't,
some of whom you can help,
maybe cherish for a while, then
easily forget.

The nurse asks if you prefer
flannelette top or bottom or both,
setting you adrift on a sea of childhood
memories, how the bed
took a long time to warm up
in winter, the determined
set of your mother's
face, the distinct attitude of her
body leaning over the machine
on Mondays, the stiffened
clatter of the sheets on the long line.

Sharp surprises: the white-haired old
man-in-the-next-bed child-like
weeps when his family comes to take him
home; a previously sullen
nurse explodes into laughter at an everyday
remark. Why? Like the fugitive elements
of a poem, like the dark swing and happenstance
of history, like the rhythmic
reciprocations of a marriage,
things come together, lock
and hold, however briefly. Then
it's gone.

The old man barely
waves to you as he
shuffles out the door.
Flannelette or cotton –
it hardly matters. Why
am I here? ("I heard he
stepped on a nail..."

May 1983

At 75 she has broken her hip in 3 places.
In the next room, until at least 2 a.m.,
she will walk the cracked and warping corridors
of memory and pain. Up out of the cloud of chemicals
they have tried to quench her with, a single
filament of trained and fading incandescence
remembers still the old formulas:

> *Holy Mary, Mother of God...*
> *Take me to Thee...*
> *O Christ, come quickly, come quickly...*

The voice wears a dress of childhood, almost
laughs, carefree in the security of the known
and ancient words. The rhythms are echoes:
priestlike, predictable.

But then a new and ardent presence overtakes her:

> *O Jesus please come for me*
> *pleeeaase o pleeeaase*
> *I want to go I can't stand*
> *why don't you come now please*
> *o please I'm soooooooo*
> *tired I can't Jesus wait pleeeaase*
> *come o...*

The tones descend into a dark low register,
turn animal yet gentle, caressing. The seemingly endless
energy in the crippled, pale body draws me in:
entranced, I strain, listening for her breath to give out at last.
Instead the keening rises to a bright whine, lifts
its tangled imprecations, its ravelled oratory,
into a fever of screams, again and again, forsaking
all dignity, terrible in their reaching...

The nurse comes then, is cross, even, in her chiding:
"You're disturbing everyone, you know, sister;
we can't have that."

But the flat new silence
is no relief.

In the morning she will not remember.
At the next evening's darkness she will start again.

Apparently she cannot die.

July 1986

LISA WITH CELLO

She does not yet know
how to play it, is just
"trying it out" as prelude
to buying it (or not),
so has carried it all the way
up to my hospital room
to show me how it looks,
how it will sound.

Carefully she removes it
from its canvas case, draws
the straight-backed chair
out from the wall,
gets into position to play.

But the floor's hard marble
will not accept the sharp spike,
so one of my slippers must be
improvised as a cushioned pad
to create a kind of stability.
Now we are ready.

She embraces the dark wood
as though they have long
been lovers – comfortable, easy, calm.

Then it happens: taking up the bow,
she makes the cello yield
its primal sounds, Unstopped, the strings
respond; the room cherishes,
holds on to, this unusual
occupancy as long as it can.

There is a still moment when I stare
past my wounded, bandaged foot
at the emerging scene: the colourless
wall, the standard dresser, the ordinary
chair. And then – she is there, regal,
commanding, united with the warm
wood, the pulsing notes. Her eyes
touch the strings where the bow
moves, listen to the intense colours.
Her lips are moving into a smile, *dolce*.

Singly or in twos the nurses
enter, drawn by this new
presence in their midst.
They stand a moment,
smile and leave.

I also smile, realize
that when we finally
change this room for home,
she will be there with cello,
and we will play *continuo*...

May 1983

Ps 46:5-12 (BCP) There is a River W.J. Barnes (1987)

S.A.T.B and Organ

for L.A.M., bright stream

Slow, flowing

the ho-ly place of the ta-ber-na-cle of the most High. ———

the ho-ly place of the ta-ber-na-cle of the most High. ———

the ho-ly place of the ta-ber-na-cle of the most High. ———

the ho-ly place of the ta-ber-na-cle of the most High. ———

God is in the midst of her, ——— there-fore shall she not ——— be moved; —

God is in the midst of her, ——— there-fore shall she not ——— be moved; —

God is in the midst of her, ——— there-fore shall she not ——— be moved; —

God is in the midst of her, ——— there-fore shall she not ——— be moved; —

Conservatory Brand   Printed in Canada   THE FREDERICK HARRIS MUSIC CO. LIMITED. OAKVILLE, CANADA

Soprano Solo:

a tempo
mp

rit.
O — come —
hi — ther, — and be-hold the works — of the Lord,

Tutti
mp what won — ders — he hath wrought up-on the earth.

mp what won — ders — he hath wrought up-on the earth.

mp what won — ders — he hath wrought up-on the earth.

mp what won — ders — he hath wrought up-on the earth.

V.S.

Conservatory Brand

Printed in Canada

THE FREDERICK HARRIS MUSIC CO. LIMITED.
OAKVILLE, CANADA

- 8 -

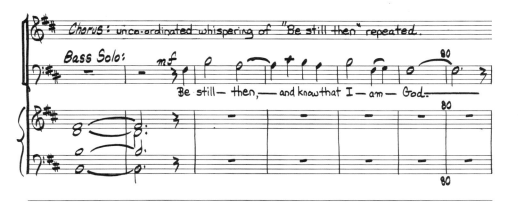

Conservatory Brand

Printed in Canada

THE FREDERICK HARRIS MUSIC CO. LIMITED.
OAKVILLE, CANADA

68

Conservatory Brand   Printed in Canada   THE FREDERICK HARRIS MUSIC CO. LIMITED.
OAKVILLE, CANADA

a — ri - ver, — the streams where-of make glad the ci-ty of God, —

a — ri - ver, — the streams where-of make glad the ci-ty of God, —

a — ri - ver, — the streams where-of make glad the ci-ty of God, —

a — ri - ver, — the streams where-of make glad the ci-ty of God, —

the ho — ly place of the ta - ber - na - cle of the most — High. —

the ho — ly place of the ta - ber - na - cle of the most — High. —

the ho — ly place of the ta - ber - na - cle of the most — High. —

the ho — ly place of the ta - ber - na - cle of the most — High. —

MARINA WITH
MOZART AT HOTEL DIEU

She is one of the new
generation of nurses: at her first
entrance into my room, she offers
easily, "Hi! My name is Marina,"
and sets about what needs doing
with an air both amateur
and professional, her lovely
olive skin fresh (or almost) as a young
child's.

The other nurses have never
told me their names. But she is still
a student, maybe twenty or twenty-one, not yet
calloused by routine, so worries about
my quickened pulse, my rising blood-pressure.

She knows everything and she knows
nothing: is not aware of the appearances
of her name in literature,
of Shakespeare's *Pericles* or Eliot's
poem, does not realize that "Marina"
is associated with sea-changes, with trial
and rebirth, with "grace
dissolved in place." But she
responds, smiling, to the *Clarinet
Quintet* on my tape-player, could
"listen to that all day,"
doesn't recognize the piece or know Mozart,
but she saw the last episode of M*A*S*H,
and used to play classical music
on her accordion.

Later, bathing and dressing my wound,
she tells me that she's Greek, that her father
died early, of cancer, that her mother
works in the kitchen of this hospital.
She says this with the quick smile
of one who has absorbed the hurt and is still
holding on.

But for now
the strains of the Mozart mingle with the warm
sounds of her voice, the clarinet
makes its energetic staccato leaps,
the strings bustle, contribute their moving
harmony.

Outside, it has been raining for two days.
In the half-light of seven-thirty a.m.
the doctor has had nothing very hopeful
to say. But now the sun
starts to find its way through the drab
mesh of the institutional curtains:
    the sun's
long fingers, Mozart's amazing
pen, the players' passionate discipline, her
smooth, her carefully competent
hands.

ECHOCARDIOGRAM
for Bruce Pond

It is a message delivered
from the cavity of my chest.

The gregarious technician has fixed electrodes,
observed his gauges, set his dials.

Now the everyday scientific wonder begins:
sound waves are translated

into a picture on the green
monitor; points of light realize

my heart. A small three-sided
opening lets me watch

that dark rooted muscle
bulge and subside, swell and contract:

thump-*thump*, thump-*thump*, thump-*thump,*
the ancient irresistible rhythm

falling in doublets, two-four time,
time and time again....

The touch of a button summons
a different view: the valves

perform their seductive two-step,
out and back, thump-*thump*.

Opening and closing thus, they become
eyes winking or mouths flirting,

drawing me in to a red secret,
which I share and do not share....

I sense that I have glimpsed
a tissued engine such as moves

in every moving thing: a gift
which has itself been given a fixed

unfathomable number of kicks.
When they are done, it stops.

Within the centre of myself I've seen
the coming and withdrawing of a god.

July 1988

ANGELICO'S MAGI

Fra Angelico,
you who were called "Beato,"

I have just been to see the piety
of your painting of the three wise men.

It was there
in the patterned gold mosaic
of the wall outside the stable,

there
in the uncomfortable prostration
of the aged king, crimson-robed,
his crown beside him on the ground,
his bearded face awaiting blessing,

there too
in the praying hands, averted eyes
of the one who stands behind him,
and in the quiet waiting of the third,
his gift held firmly by ten regal fingers.

Their postures, gestures, eyes
lead me to those others:
Joseph holding a gift,
Mary the child, the latter not
(as with some other artists)
receiving gold but reaching out
to touch that balding head, those wisps of white.

Joseph and Mary have in their eyes
the joy that holds them there
in deep solemnity,
and the Child seems to look
right through this royal discomfort
of an old man at his feet,
toward some future ...

I saw all that. I understood.

Then, to the right, the retinue,
the courtly followers of these splendid kings,
nodding and whispering, pointing to the star
and at each other,
only a step from glory,
excited, multi-coloured, individuals...

I knew why they were there.

But I was puzzled for a moment
by a small detail:

behind these men of station,
in the top right corner
(directly opposite that other corner
where the golden star appears)
there stands a youthful groom,
his back toward us,
tugging the bridle of an unruly horse.

One hand struggles with the rampant bit;
the other arm, rich-liveried, reaches back
beside the golden hair streaming
from his upraised head,

and in that hand the handle
of what seems to be
(though almost blocked out
by a shoulder) a whip:

the lad is about to strike.

I know it is a small detail
and in the background, so to speak,
but being there
it tells us more
about your piety
than "Beato"
or "Angelico"
ever could.

QUAESTIONES DEO

I

I sit upon the rock-face, which is being
assaulted by the waves' hammering,
admiring as always
the stability of anything stable
(worrying at the same time also
about the relentlessness of water in motion).

But (to keep to the rock)
I remember that some have seen it
loyal and majestic –
one could even say adamant –
doing now as always
what few of us have done for very long
since Adam.

And that's nice too,
I tell myself,
but then I wonder
as I sit here
Just what loyalty can mean to rock,
what will it has to work its life,
and where, if (as the theory goes)
all things are growing up to God,
the rock comes in...

If we, who have our persons near us now,
are right to think we may expect
some "higher form of personality-relationship,"
how will the rock achieve its face,
and when?

The question's not so hard
with birds, or even trees;
the trouble is to find
a grand maturity for rock...

And if imagination can't conceive
this rock-transforming change,
how can I think so easily
a different, new-made me?

If rocky nature is as hard for you
as it is for me,
what will you do with mine?

II

Up from the cracks and scars along the rock,
where I can see no soil, nothing at all,
are growing
not just the cedars
with their scrawny, clutching fingers of root,
but the flowers
also,
delicate thrusts of yellow and purple and red,
having made their own green for backdrop,
asserting as they seem to do
not merely the ubiquitous, almost inevitable
reaching of life,
but the supererogatory fragrance
of beauty, too...

I have learned from learned friends
that before the cedars and the flowers
were the mosses,
and before them were the lichens,
in a procession that leads me
back to the rock,
but doesn't explain it.

For I know also
(if only from their numbers)
that this way to the flowers
must have been the hardest,
least inevitable,
most capricious.

So that when I now look down
upon this yellow
or this purple
or this red,
my mind insists on asking
what the fragrance of the flower means.

(Another part of me
is tempted to reply
something about the fragrance of the flower
being by itself enough...
but I can't.)

And so I say
that what the flower says
is certainly, I think,
that beauty's never had without great cost,
or that something can be done with even rock
if you know how,
– which satisfies the mind enough for now,
permitting as it does
analogy to human things.

what I am too afraid to ask
in public, so to speak,
(and maybe much too faithless, too)
is whether in this order
that I see proceeding here,
as it leads me back to rock,
there is nothing more
than rock plus lichens,
plus the mosses,
plus the rest,
where no-one knew –
or cared to know –
just what was coming next.

Suppose the answer to the question, then, were
yes,
what would it have to say
to what I think I know of you?

And as for me
(to think no simple after-thought)
would this all mean
that all my meaning
is in me? And how could I
stand up
beside the flowers?

LEAVING DAMASCUS*

No flying carpet, this, no freakish bald
giant coaxed from a lamp to execute
the three commands, no magic wand to waft
you out of this new bind and whisk you away.

Instead, an ordinary basket made of reeds
(a kind of trunk? a clothes-hamper?) stands near
at hand and does the trick. The strands are woven,
criss-crossed for strength, and there's no more than room
enough for even your small body, cramped
and awkward, as the others tie down the lid,
the cut edges of reeds pricking your flesh.

But it works: under darkness, through the thin
window, the guts of friends are ropes paid out
to let you down and set you free again.

July 1986

*See Acts 9:25 and 2 Corinthians 11:33.

Words by
George Herbert (1593-1633) Love Bade Me Welcome W. J. Barnes (July 1989)

S.A.T.B. and Organ

For Mollie and Bob Brow

S [a cappella]

mp 1. Love bade me wel—come——, yet my soul—drew back—, guil-ty of dust and sinne.

A

mp 1. Love bade me wel—come—— , yet my soul—drew back—, guil-ty of dust and sinne.

T

mp 1. Love bade me wel—come——, yet my soul—drew back—, guil-ty of dust and sinne.

B

mp 1. Love bade me wel—come——, yet my soul—drew back—, guil-ty of dust and sinne.

[Organ tacet]

mf But quick-ey'd Love, ob-serv-ing me grow slack from my first en-trance in——, drew

mf But quick-ey'd Love, ob-serv-ing me grow slack from my first en-trance in——, drew

mf But quick-ey'd Love, ob-serv-ing me grow slack from my first en-trance in——, drew

mf But quick-ey'd Love, ob-serv-ing me grow slack from my first en-trance in——, drew

Mayfair MUSIC
2600 John St. Unit 209, Markham, Ont. L3R 2W4

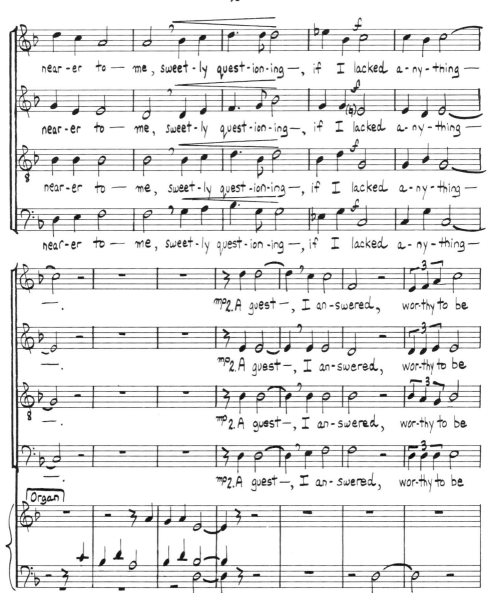

near-er to — me, sweet-ly quest-ion-ing —, if I lacked a-ny-thing —

near-er to — me, sweet-ly quest-ion-ing —, if I lacked a-ny-thing —

near-er to — me, sweet-ly quest-ion-ing —, if I lacked a-ny-thing —

near-er to — me, sweet-ly quest-ion-ing —, if I lacked a-ny-thing —

—. *mp* 2. A guest—, I an-swered, wor-thy to be

—. *mp* 2. A guest—, I an-swered, wor-thy to be

—. *mp* 2. A guest—, I an-swered, wor-thy to be

—. *mp* 2. A guest—, I an-swered, wor-thy to be

Organ

Mayfair MUSIC
2600 John St. Unit 209, Markham, Ont. L3R 2W4

Our Lady is not dead:
    with what wonder
Do I see her reach this hand which cradles mine
And with that free serenity of hers
Proffer this quiet look, this brightening sign
Of many births, small worlds advanced,
If only for this moment: still enough
(Given my situation) to have lanced
Old flesh with gratitude, access of love
Not looked for.
    But, she and that lovely child
Not being here as you are, you must take
The song which she and he and you so mild
Require.
    Accept it easy for your sake,
And for my need to see the slow release
Of beauty's worrying fancy into peace.

OPEN LETTER TO * * *

Sir, I thought you'd probably like to know
how much I marvel how you could have
(in the midst of all the things going
on just now; I mean, what with Nigeria-
Biafra, Vietnam, the Middle
East, to mention only the biggest;
then, of course, the race
riots, violent confrontations left
and right, and the usual father against
usual son, multiplied endlessly; and, besides
that, all those people bringing their
individual problems; you know:
basketball players at the foul line crossing
themselves, drivers wanting to get
home O.K., their Christopher medals now
obsolete, mothers looking out for their
kids, some priest readying a man for the electric
chair, a child wanting everything,
an alcoholic asking will-power for the thirty-
ninth time, old ladies needlessly seeking self-
control, farmers wanting rain, or no rain, unions
a better deal, and maybe a couple of million
others just out after the strength to get through another
day, a few thousand maybe here and there longing
for death, not an easy question certainly
found the time, whatever particle it took
from your eternity, not to mention your energy,
to have the thought and make it happen,
bringing her here to me.

TO A BEAUTIFUL LADY,
AFTER TALK AND SLEEP

God, woman,
when I look
at you,
I wish I were both
Petrarc and Sidney.

And,
except for the fact
that I'm having trouble
writing poems,
I am.

JUXTAPOSITIONS

There lies
that stack of books
upon my desk,
the covers proof
against all union.

And so nothing of *Life*
On The Mississippi
gets through to mingle with *Sex*
in Christianity and Psychoanalysis.

Nor can *The History of the Kiss*
reach down to taste
of Bridge's *Testament of Beauty.*

And *Modern English Usage*
sends no hosts of words
to parle with Spenser's
Faerie Queene.

By reason of their boundaries
of paper, cardboard, cloth,
these bodies merely touch.

Here, then, another lesson
in the mysteries of love,
here yet another way
to see that you and I
together are the more alive:

for even if we had
no waking words
to figure forth our hearts,

I still would know,
would still recall,

that when we lie asleep,
your body close to mine,

the currents
of our fleshed
articulations
flow on
still.

FOR SUSAN, LEAVING

After the flat meadow,
after the cool shade of pines,
turning, how suddenly have we found
this old, decaying mill
standing bewildered,
awkward about what to make
of this unusual motion at its heart:

spring rains explode the mill-stream,
which in this morning sunlight
surges fire against the stone,
flashes profitless down the race,
being only beautiful as it goes.

And I guess that we are like that –
no useful purpose in this moment,
except its beautiful sad rushing
towards its end.

I know that the magnificence here
is strong yet wasting,
know that summer's even heat
will shrink this fiery whiteness
back to earth again,
leaving a dilapidated mill,
so briefly graced.

I know this.

And yet another part of me
would ask a second gift:

that we might go still further on
to where analogy would find an end.

But trepidation of the spheares,
Though greater farre, is innocent.

we are all sublunary these days, though:
everything fluid from the beginning: moons
banging around inside the brain-pan,
splotches of half-light rounding,
crescents popping and forming, reeling and sliding
off the edges of the screen, a trembling
as at great heights, splinters of moonray
stuck in the throat, shadows leaving only
to come again.

Sphere-chime gone into time now,
the amazement's how the innocence
remains, stays in the eyeball's little
universe, complete though inexact:
how glimpse and touch,
fine hair and warm places,
keep time with a strange and final purity,
move free from guilt's long
finger-point and curiously hold.

There's a meeting that comes hard
upon the pace of now,
that opens softnesses, and mines
a darkness always there: and we
can only take the heart's
irregular motions, not refuse
the dancing circle of this quickening place.

SPRING SONG

Some things are *not* best left unsaid, undone:
Under a disturbing sun, the trees are leaving again.
Elements quicken toward another ending.

Does it seem senseless that the long dark hair
Answers me nothing, above the red sweater,
Nor encourages a green thought ...

Doors close on startled eyes.
Over and over, a voice I hope uncertain, saying No.

Everything must hold to the moment
Left to it: we are found always
In caressing a legacy from where time does not matter,
Zany as it may seem in prospect or in retrospect.
And in the end there is no refuge or retreat
Besides acceptance, which is always possible.
Ends are for starting from, a way of travelling
That enables confidence,
Hanging on.

Reality makes concessions, though;
All natural gifts may be refused,
Though you must know that even unreadiness
Has, in the troubled history of love, been loved,
But for the present I can hope that you will, through the madness,
Undertake the cherishing,
Not turn away.

THE MAKER

His love had tried to teach her flesh a poem
And so, by entertaining various ways,
Provide an ardent mirror without frame
Able to testify how lovely she
Might be forever, and in this more free.

But she refused to contemplate his craft,
Perhaps could not endure its scrutiny,
So turned away and fell asleep; and left
Him baffled by her desolate prisoned ways
Until a poem burnt them into praise.

AFTERWORD

Awkwardly, as if two
self-conscious strangers meeting
by previous arrangement, almost as if
in proxy for others, meeting
with flowers in their lapels
to know each other by
(or perhaps a wild bright tie)
in a bus terminal somewhere,

we come together, your thin arms
encumbered with your books
(Milton included)
barricading between us,

for this first kiss
(which you say
is also to be our last)

and just as awkwardly
come apart,
straightening ourselves
to do business as instructed,
with no time now to look for faces,

I picking up suit-cases, so to speak,
and leading you across public concourses again,
aware of the cabbies staring,
making my talk small.

I will not tell you now,
but you will someday come
to know there is with me
a history of awkwardness.

By then, though,
you will have realized
it was today
that I began unwriting
that absurd biography.

So for the moment
I accept your terms.

POEM

small Easter
        flowers
   were

smuggled out of the country
     last
        night

we should
      pass
more laws

POEM FOR LYNN,
WHO CARED AND ASKED

it was most unlikely,
I thought at the time,
not what one looked for,
not what one might have expected.

    (does he still move
    mysteriously?)

I will remember always
how you
got out of that faded
two-tone green
Rambler, you
and your daughter,
and how your slight body
came across the lawn
and how your face
gave us all that smile
which is now a part of my eyes.

    dare I ever tell you
    what I thought then?

now, here we are
circling round and round
this question which refuses
to leave either of us alone,
this question which has now become
an only-sometimes-sad
recurring joke between us.

    or rather I circle,
    for you, with what I see
    as an unusual stability,
    come right
    to the centre

    Lady
    it is a stateliness, a majesty
    which those who have known you only slightly
    cannot know at all.

but still there are many questions, here, of course
    (they are bred, sir,
    out of your mud, sir,
    by the operation
    of your sun)
and they ask a lot
of me:

how can one measure
the thrust of fear, or how
assess the frailty
of an uncertain love,
or whether another love
can hold it?

why do I always turn this over
in my mind
seeking a label
which will say
"Made In Heaven, Approved"
since I had thought
I'd given up
such tenuous cliches,
at least had learned
that what has been made there
must always be
made again on earth?

and why could I not write
this poem that you asked for
till you sent me one of yours?

    and having started now, I find
    no easy way to end

    except to say (can he be listening?)

it seems much less unlikely
now

EPIPHANY
for Elizabeth

O wise
proprietors
of that cheap
motel where I was forced
to stay the night
                    without you

(the blizzard kept the room
so cold)

: checking as always
into every corner, every drawer
(having already packed away
the free stationery
the unneeded bars
of soap)

I found

that they
had prudently provided
in the left-hand corner
of the old desk's left-hand drawer
a Gideon Bible and a prophylactic

and armed against all disaster
I smiled to think
I would encounter none
and needed no defence

till later, sleeping fitfully
I turned to embrace the truth

that empty pillow.

WORDS FOR ELIZABETH

look, love:

how everywhere your eyes go
there is dancing
there's a sparkling
there is life

& your small hands
hold acres of sunwarm
& autumn fire

& your heart i know
holds earthly much
holds many
holds me

& today we've come to this:
       published our hands
       worded our hearts
       looked our eyes:

there can be
no taking of this
our taking of each other

let every day be this day:
dance & sparkle
hold earth, hold sun, hold fire

let me keep
your hands
your eyes
your heart

let us hold our life
& so together help
keep death away
keep death away

7 October 1972

A WALK BY THE LAKE

"But marriage is essentially hopeful."
Joseph Braddock, *The Bridal Bed*

Sun recedes,
prompting the temporary
inrush of intemperate eden
into this pleasant park
where lovers, most of them
college students,
display themselves amid
the darkening greenery awhile,
linked arm to waist
or pressed together,
not waiting for full evening
to confer its anonymity,
careless, in their preoccupations,
of the hurt they do.

Together now we watch them
or I at least watch,
for you are shivering
in the breeze from off the lake
(and without remedy:
for we have moved beyond
huddling together for warmth in public)
and I know that you are worrying
about the competence of a baby-sitter.

Still, my two eyes cannot
detach themselves from this;
I am bound, like the paid janitor
of some unused factory,
to tidy up what needs no tidying,
to check that things are where I know they are.

(Gently the waves kiss those rocks,
the trees provide their canopy,
and seagulls tease the wind.)

Why have we come here?
That dinner and the wine
ought to have taken us home again satisfied.
What fond impulse stretched the evening to this madness,
this sad uncomfortable walking by the lake?

And worse, what fruitless yearning urges me
to analyze calamities,
articulate what's always been unsaid,
and raise these buried questions?

And yet this wondering holds me, and this anger.
How erase the letters on this manuscript?
What cant and nonsense Augustine spoke who raved
of freedom perfect in the slavery to God!
And why am I, some spineless Provencal,
indentured to your service, why are you
in my thinking always linked with God,
since I have come to wonder whether
either of you wants it that way very much?

How much the burden
of this lonely journey
were we given,
how much took?

It is no comfort to me now to think
that when we're safely home again
I'll try to make this into poetry
and warm you with my kiss.

POEM FOR FALL

Late autumn trees I drive past every day
I notice now again.

Against grey sky they hold
to the flooded, cooling earth:
giant's hands,
gnarled, broken, monstrous,
clutching that sky which yields them nothing,
pleading for winter to turn its face,
despite the rooted knowledge of that vanity.

With us, now, it is different:
I am no giant certainly,
and my perennial wisdom
is exploded by your smile.

Come, lady, with me now:
Ask this brave sun how he has power to brace
The frozen stillness of this January noon.
Hold always to his answer: yes,
Even when I have gone (and I must go)
Reach into given beauty. Crafted fine and strong
I have known it; it is yours.
Nor can fierce weathering take it,
Even through hosts of January days.

HOMAGE TO THEO

I would sing constellations
And start planets from my mouth,
Liberating the stars into words.

I would articulate rivers
And make orations of soaring birds,
My tongue caressing lilies also
And green roses.

I would pronounce sadnesses
And elucidate joy,
My voice persuading sunlight into the valleys.

I would compose universes entire
And tell all men their force,
Instructing my words to observe suffering.

And I would supplicate
All lovely earth and bleeding sky
To engraft their voices,
Calling for high accompaniment,
Waking the blessed from their proper love,
Enticing powers everywhere,
Seducing God even.

And, had I the courage,
I would reveal myself as one
Made vocal by your love.

Had I the courage,
I would reflect aloud
Upon your name,
Offering to other men
Its grace.

MOVING

Bright harbinger of a
rare and racing future,
you bring to me love's
nest of boxes, intricate, arcane.

Hello. I can see that you were
already here (having
remembered what's coming, not
refusing the past's odd audit)
in the fierce and fiery,
sad and maybe only seeming now.

February 1986

SUNSTRUCK

Bones bake on the parched plain;
every hour, the dark
cormorants scrape the sky,
keening the dearth of carrion;
yellow sand yields nothing.

Having once held light in our fragile flesh,
are we forever unable to give up
love's hesitant possibilities,
viewing even the sour ashes
of relinquishment as a sign
resplendent, stirring
somehow our longest memories –
of something which no blow can break
nor wretched circumstances touch?

August 1988

TWO PHOTOGRAPHS
for Marion

You, sitting on burnt grass,
trees crouching behind you,
your legs tucked under,
skirt pulled down
to cover your knees –
you, a little shy,
smiling.

A young man,
round face shiny
and glowing red
under an unseen sun,
a young man in uniform
presenting arms;
the sling of the rifle
is white, bright,
stiff.

Years later,
still a young man,
hammering on your thin
apartment door, bending
to glare through the mail-slot,
he will want to kill me,
will hardly be talked down. . . .

In the thrust and pound
of history, you and he have always been
conspiring to invade my peace,
and to see this is to be
voyeur of feverish strategems,
gathering and ready to destroy.

I stare and stare at these two photographs,
these two hard burning moments
which were aimed and waiting
in the camera's careful
and inevitable eye.

(1971-1989)

Let Us Now Praise Famous Men

Eccl. 44

W. J. Barnes

men —— re- nowned for their

power ——————.　Lead-ers of the peo -ple by their

A little slower

counsels and by their know—ledge, Such — as— found out— mu·si·cal

tunes —, and re·ci — ted ver·ses in wri·ting—;

And some there be — which have — no — me-mo-ri-al—, who — are — per — ish'd — as — though — they—had — ne — ver been—.

1972

When Mary the Mother kissed the Child

Charles G. D. Roberts

W. J. Barnes

for David Helwig

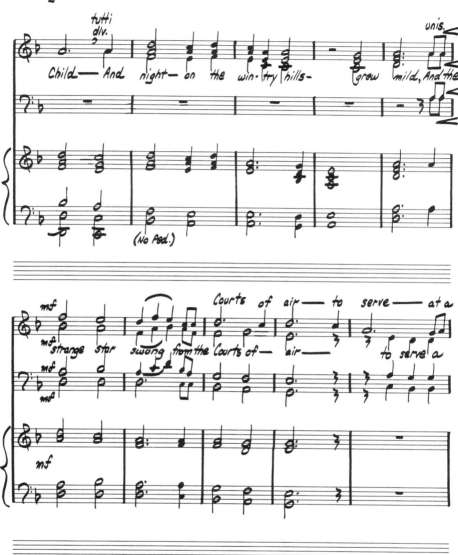

When Mary 4

121

When Mary 5

When Mary 6

pp when Ma-ry the Mo-ther gave of her breast

—to the poor inn's la-test and low-liest guest [The God born out of the wo-man's side The

[Soli

Soli

tutti

Babe of Heav-en by Earth de-nied

Then did the

tutti

hurt ones cease to moan — and the long sup-plant-ed — come to their own —.

when Mary 8

And nought to her were the kneel-ing kings, The 'ser-ving star—, And the half-seen Things,

Then was the lit-tle of earth made great — And the man came back—to the God's — e-

state ——— . P   When Ma — ry the Mo·ther — kissed the P Child —

July · August 1981

Stand where the place is.
Stand where the place will be.

Whether this blue-jay flies away
or rests its flight,
     I will be here.

And whether the trilliums
in my meadows drop,
whether the clouds allow
the moon its path or not,
     I will be here.

Or whether my generous daughter
gives her beauty all away,
     I will be father still.

Or if disease unfolds
and cancers boil under the skin
and wrinkles crowd the eye,
     I will remain.

Whether with bony regularity
white-knuckled crowds beat savagely,
     I will be here.

And when the child I knew is shattered
in a gas-exploded room,
     I will remain.

Or uncles and aunts go falling into earth
or motorcycled limbs crash into pavement
ending the music of a young man's life,
     I will be here.

And whether you my love
should go or stay, taking or leaving
all that is my good,
     I will be here still.

With all my strength and weakness
let me say it:

    I will remain
    I must be here
    I must

holding a face uneasily toward this hour

preparing the standard welcome for the end.

A KIND OF ELEGY

Winter persists into April
This mottled afternoon
        As we drive north
To a small village
Where we will put into the ground
        The body of the young man
Who moved so easily among us
Until two nights ago
        When he hanged himself

Flanked by a quantity of evergreens
A large red billboard
        Offering in yellow letters
Life insurance through an independent agent
        Passes.

And I remember
How last night at suppertime my daughter
        Seemed to be growing so fast,
So pretty her face and so meaningful her talk
As she reached out to touch and explore
The funny hairs upon my cheek,
        And there were about her
All the signs of the beginning
        Of a ravishing maturity.

And I remembered Yeats's prayer
And I wished he were alive and here
        So I could spit upon him
For wanting all those towered walls
Behind which he could watch exfoliate
        His carefully encultured flower:
Petals protected against all shock
        But not against all withering.

Let then my daughter not refuse
        The wreck
Of the warm gesture proffered,
Nor encase in the wrappings of carefulness
        Her heart
When it later moves
As naturally as it does now
        In curiosity and affection.

Let her not hope to hold
        Her beauty without excess,
Nor worry much about what men
Have in their wisdom called
        Integrity.

Let her rather take the wind
        For company
And entertain unquietness
        When prompted.
Send her a lover who can learn,
        Accept from her,
That here is no longer soil
For deeper roots
        As Yeats once longed for.

And when it is all over
        Let her come
Suffering to You still suffering.
Take her to You as gently as can be,
        Still in her curious hand
        Still closely held
Such hands as these
        That clutch the dust.